MY CUP OVERFLOWS
... with grace unseen

A POETRY COLLECTION

CHINCHU KURIAKOSE

BookLeaf Publishing

India | USA | UK

Presentation by *BookLeaf Publishing*

Web: www.bookleafpub.com
E-mail: info@bookleafpub.com

ISBN: 9789369533039

First edition 2025

DEDICATION

I dedicate my book to my nephew Ethan, the newest member of our family. He is our toddler explorer; the way his eyes sparkle in wonder every time he finds something new, I connect to the same wonder every time a story or a thought strikes me.

CONTENTS

A GRATITUDE NOTE

I thank you, my dear Lord, for your abundance of grace in my life through gifts, people, blessings and circumstances.

"My grace is sufficient for you, for my power is made perfect in weakness." ~ 2 Corinthians 12:9

The above verse sums it all up for me.

My family, friends, teachers, readers, and well-wishers—having the right support system around me despite my imperfections and weaknesses—enable me to explore my passion.

FOREWORD

It is said that the poetical language of an age should be the current language heightened. This is all the more true for Chinchu Kuriakose's poems, which get elevated from the plight of the word of common parlance to the divine heights of sublimity transcending the barriers of the confinement of the very limited meaning of the word and reaching a realm of the hitherto inexperienced thoughts and experiences. As Timothy Steele once said: *All the fun is in how you say a thing.* Chinchu really understands the essence of this saying; she absorbs its spirit and is able to express things in a different way. This perspective makes all the difference and helps her poems to stand apart.

When Chinchu speaks of a journey down the hill, it ceases to be a mere travel and imbibes the ecstasies and agonies of a sojourn that can be defined as life. Her poem 'My Adventure with you' is agog with the echoes of different meanings that resonate the attributes of life through a plethora of original images and innovative concepts. These elements transform a simple collection of words into a meaningful poem, taking us to a celestial world of newer sensibilities that renew the soul of the reader afresh.

She speaks through images, rather than words and this is how a truly poetic mind unfolds. The poem 'Meditation' captures the essence of meditation, introspection, and the journey towards inner peace through vivid, contemplative imagery and a calming rhythm. The speaker's experience of sitting on a yoga mat, aligning body and mind, and eventually letting go of worldly distractions to achieve stillness reflects a universal search for balance amidst life's transience.

For the poet, the poetic sojourn is an extension from tradition to modernity. At times, it reaches the highly noble level of supreme poetic utterances, making the reader undergo a real purge, both physically and spiritually. It makes all the difference.

The poem 'Home' deserves a special mention. This poem beautifully captures the warmth, comfort, and irreplaceable significance of home. Beginning with the imagery of "crisp white cotton" sheets and the "aroma of freshly brewed coffee," it immediately evokes a cozy, familiar setting. The poet contrasts the societal expectation to adapt ("be like Romans while in Rome") with the sense of sovereignty felt in one's own space, where they are "the kings". The mother's care heightens this sense of belonging, illustrating home as a nurturing, sacred space where they can be their most authentic self. The closing lines resonate deeply, portraying home as a lasting resort and a place of ultimate return.

Why do we write? Is it for honours, prizes or accolades? Had it been so, Geoffrey Chaucer would not have attempted to scribble down a hefty work such as *The Canterbury Tales*, as in his era, no award was instituted by the authorities or by any other literary institution. A heavy heart has no option, but to weep, a bud that can't resist its inner urge has no option but to bloom, and a tearful mind has no option, but to melt into tears. Thus, poems come to the heart of Chinchu quite naturally—instinctively, instantaneously and spontaneously.

It is an amalgamation of two different cultures, a confluence of the Eastern and the Western, both strictly traditional and lucidly modern. Above all, what I feel in these lines of poetry is nothing other than the throb of a heart that longs for a listener, the weeping of a solitary soul that longs for a source of solace. However, in a world of varying styles and schools of poetry, Chinchu's voice here stands out distinctively.

This collection of poems is a masterful fusion of contrasting cultures—a convergence of the East's profound heritage with the West's flowing modernity, a delicate dance between heritage and novelty. Beneath the poetic lines lies the unmistakable heartbeat of a soul reaching out, a voice steeped in solitude yet longing for understanding and solace. Each verse pulses with the yearnings of a solitary spirit, drawing in the listener with an almost palpable depth of feeling. In the vast expanse of poetic voices, where countless forms and schools weave diverse tapestries, Chinchu's voice resounds uniquely, vividly and unmistakably, captivating and compelling the world to listen.

—Prabha Varma- Poet, Lyricist, Journalist

A voracious writer with poems, novels, books on the contemporary socio-political milieu and literature, six collections of essays in criticism, a study on media, a travelogue and a novel in English. Recipient of many awards, including the prestigious Saraswathi Samman for 2023 for his work Roudra Sathwikam, a novel in verse. (Saraswathi Samman is an annual award for outstanding prose or poetry literary works in any of the 22 languages of India listed in the Constitution of India).

THROUGH A TEACHER'S EYES

I feel privileged to present this collection of poems penned by one of my gifted students, whose voice, imagination, and insight shine through each line. Poetry, in its purest form, is a reflection of the heart and mind, capturing the subtle beauty of human experience and the richness of life's emotions. In these pages, you will find a tapestry of thoughts, woven with a keen sense of observation and a deep sensitivity that is rare for someone so young.

This collection speaks of universal themes—love, hope, resilience, and the wonder of the world around us—expressed with a freshness and honesty that is both refreshing and inspiring. Each poem invites readers to pause and reflect, to see the world through the eyes of youth, and to appreciate the nuances of life often overlooked in our hurried lives.

As you journey through this collection, I encourage you to take time with each piece, allowing the words to resonate and stir. These poems are a testament to the boundless creativity that resides in each student and a reminder of the importance of nurturing young voices. May this collection not only showcase the talent of a promising poet but also inspire others to find their own creative expression.

Reflecting on Chinchu's journey from a young student in my class to a published poetess fills me with profound pride and admiration. During her school years, I never noticed glimpses of her potential and I never anticipated that she would blossom into such a gifted writer. "Mea culpa, mea culpa, mea maxima culpa". Now, as a young adult, she has not only discovered her voice but also mastered the art of weaving emotions into words, touching readers' hearts and minds. Watching her creative evolution has been a privilege, a testament to the beauty of nurturing talent and seeing it come to fruition.

Her first book, *A Teaspoonful of Life,* was a remarkable achievement in itself, but now, with the publication of her second work, *My Cup Overflows...* with Grace Unseen, she has truly established herself as an accomplished poetess. This journey from a quiet schoolgirl to a published author is inspiring, both for those who know her and for aspiring writers everywhere. It's a rare joy when someone we once guided as a teacher grows before our eyes into a person of talent and depth, crafting her own path. Such transformations remind us of the potential that lies dormant within each young mind, waiting to be discovered, nurtured, and shared with the world. Chinchu's growth is not only a personal achievement but also a gift to those of us who have had the privilege of witnessing it. In the pages that follow, I invite you to journey alongside me through a tapestry of emotions, experiences, and reflections, all woven together by the threads of poetry.

"My Adventure with You" is more than just a poem; it is a celebration of connection—between lovers, friends, and the self. Each poem is a stepping stone on this path of exploration, revealing the beauty and complexity of our shared human experience.

As we traverse through themes of love, trust, and introspection, you will encounter moments of vulnerability and strength. From the comfort of home to the depths of longing, these poems encapsulate the myriad ways we navigate our relationships with one another and with ourselves. They echo the whispers of our hearts, the lessons learned through trials, and the joy found in simple moments.

The poem, "More than I can Remember" beautifully captures the introspective journey of a nurse as she contemplates the countless lives she has touched through her work. Each stanza introduces a new element of nature—a breeze, stream, goldfinch, dew drop, butterfly—that poses the same question: "How many lives have you touched?" The repeated answer, "More than I can remember," reflects the quiet yet profound impact of her role, emphasizing how often her care is extended, unnoticed, yet deeply felt. In the final stanza, the nurse herself, dressed in her uniform, embodies the answer—she has touched lives beyond measure. This poem is a touching tribute to the selfless dedication of nurses, who, like the elements in nature, quietly nurture and support life in immeasurable ways. It's autobiographical.

I hope these verses resonate with you, sparking reflections of your own adventures, the faces that have graced your path, and the lessons that have shaped your story. May you find solace, inspiration, and perhaps a piece of your own journey within these words.

Thank you for joining me in this exploration. Together, let us celebrate the adventure of life, love, and all that lies in these lines.

—A R Girija Devi, Educationalist, CEO, ELL Phonics, Trivandrum

AUTHOR'S NOTE

My Cup Overflows with Grace Unseen is my second Anthology, after *A Teaspoonful of Life*.

Inspired by Psalms 23, I named my anthology *My Cup Overflows with Grace Unseen*. This choice was not arbitrary but deeply rooted in my personal history.

My mother told me that the first words I ever learned and wrote were from Psalms 23. This early connection to the scripture has since influenced my life and work. So, the title could be considered a manifestation of God's will or just a coincidence, depending on how you interpret it.

I see stories in everything around me. They swirl in my thoughts and spill out as words. Sometimes, these words invade me, like a sudden downpour, taking over and guiding my thoughts and actions. In these moments, I happily let go of myself, allowing the words to captivate me and lead me on a journey of self-discovery.

Words transform as they travel from the writer to the reader, connecting differently with each reader.

My Cup Overflows with Grace Unseen is a profoundly personal collection of thoughts I wrote last year. It includes my observations of life—the joy I experienced, the sights I beheld, the people I encountered, the stories I absorbed, moments of gratitude, faith, inner conflicts, and more.

The collection subtly embraces the simplicities and complexities of life. Though the emotions and feelings are profoundly personal, you might find a poem that resonates with you or with someone you know—or perhaps none at all. Whatever the case, enjoy reading and keep smiling.

**Much love and God bless,
Chinchu Kuriakose**

1

MY ADVENTURE
WITH YOU!!

The path got tricky as we walked,

"Keep moving," was all that you said.

Still keeping our hands interlocked,

I kept following you to where you led.

Later, we reached greener grounds,

This time, we walked hand in hand.

It is much easier than how it sounds,

For a life that never goes as planned.

And the time came for us to climb,

You tied me to you and pulled me up.

Though the rock was wet with slime,

With you, it felt like another gallop.

It was our turn now to walk downhill,

"Don't look down," you said; I obeyed.

The air gave a bone-cracking chill,

Yet my eyes on you never swayed.

The alleys that were walked by us two,

Tell me of the trust you've earned.

I wouldn't have done it without you,

For this love and the lessons learned.

You'd think I know you well by now,

But each day, I discover a newer you.

You keep up with it, I don't know how,

For being my adventure, that you do.

MUSING

Reflection is an essential part of my professional and personal life. It helps me improve, understand myself deeply, and better appreciate how far I have come. "My Adventure with you" is such a reflection I did on our Eleventh Wedding Anniversary. Do you look back and reflect on your life, folks?

2

A BIRD TALK

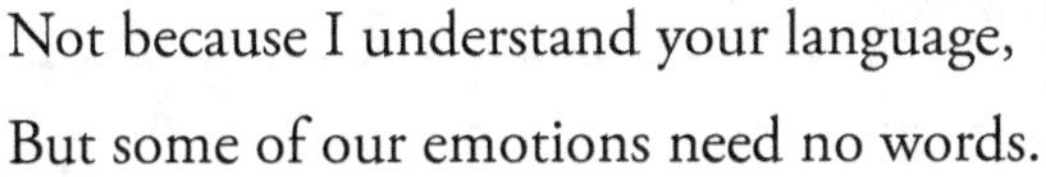

Don't be scared, birdie; I am
just a friend,

I can read your thoughts from
your eyes

Not because I understand your language,

But some of our emotions need no words.

We are from different worlds, I do know,

But I, too, feel terrified, just like you do.

Deceived by people who smile to my face,

But utter hurtful words behind my back.

Trust is such a thing we can't live without,

Once lost, it is difficult to build back again.

No matter how much we try, a fear remains,

As these are lessons, we learn the hard way.

I'm neither a hunter, nor are you my prey

So, let us leave those trust issues behind.

You belong to this world as much as I do,

Let's share the space and everything in it.

See the grains in my open palm, my dear,

Your beak looks sharp, but I'll let you peck.

With the belief that you do me no harm,

In the same way, you stay and not fly away.

MUSING

Birdwatching is a pastime I enjoy when I am home. I leave food and water in the garden; there are regular and occasional visitors. This beautiful thought arose from an encounter with a pigeon, to whom I offered grains from my hand. She didn't fly away, but she didn't peck the grain in my hand either. Didn't she trust me? Was it because her beak was sharp and she didn't want to hurt me? I often wonder what birds and animals think—do they even think at all? They instinctively know how to stay safe, but do they ever feel insecure like we do?

THANK YOU, MISS

A lesson awaits us every day to learn,
It could be a skill or a new technique.
And that makes you think and reflect,
Have we always been good learners?

I know we didn't come all set and built,
We've always been curious and eager.
No doubt we looked around in wonder,
And astonished at the *hows* and *whys*.

We were once children, all bewildered,
We were keen and sometimes scared.
But we learned to reason and resolve,
With a confidence we never had before.

When you look in the mirror each day,

Are you proud of the person you see?

What you see is indeed a work of art,

Where your teachers play a vital part.

Aren't we a blessed lot, my dear folks?

Raised by our excellent teachers.

Who sowed the seeds of wisdom in us,

And a craving to learn rooted deep within.

MUSING

We never stop learning in life. Learning starts at home and then continues in school. It doesn't stop even after we leave school because we are all trained to face life lessons independently by then. The people who mould us into who we are now are our teachers. Every culture respects teachers, especially Indian Culture; we also celebrate them on the 5th of September, Teacher's Day. This thought is a tribute to my excellent teachers who made me who I am today. I sent this to one of my teachers, and her response was something I would cherish for life.

4

STREETLIGHTS

As it starts to get dark, a warm
glow fills the street,

It's like a familiar mystic tale,
once again on repeat.

The beauty of light is
understood better in its absence,

As it imparts a better view through a different lens.

I love streetlights; strangely enough, I should admit,

It has nothing to do with the orange light they emit.

As it fills the air with romance on our couple walks,

By adding colour and gentleness to our happy talks.

Streetlights are like guardian angels; I often feel,

Leading me all the way home, and it's no big deal.

In the dark of the night, a kind of reassurance reveals,

It forms a halo, or is it an aura where my fear conceals?

I stood by the lamppost, with the love of my life,

Enjoying a chat where there is no room for strife.

Watching the reflection of light, an art to my eyes,

As if it screams, that is where all the beauty lies.

MUSING

It was a wonderful autumn evening spent at the Village Hall, where our friends were doing some rehearsals for an upcoming programme. Once everyone left, a few children waited for their parents to come and pick them up. As we waited outside, the children formed groups and conversed while my husband and I admired the streetlights. I am amazed at how little things like the beauty of autumn, the halo of lights, the misty haze, and the night's noises impart such joy and creativity with their magnificence.

5

THE CLOCK TOWER
(THE BIG BEN)

The clang of bells stopped me
from taking another step,

My sudden halt disrupted the
flowing crowd.

A man walking his dog stepped
on me, earning a yelp

The voice got absorbed in the
horde, as it wasn't loud.

I looked up to the beauty captured before my eyes,

The clock tower that stood gleaming in the sun.

With dusk approaching, a blush spread across the skies,

Which I couldn't help admiring, and I wasn't done.

The streets of London always have a story to tell,

Of the cosmopolitan taste and cheering city lights.

The city itself has a halo around casting its spell,

That keeps glowing like fireflies on dark winter nights.

London, I can't help but love you with all my heart,

For that young girl from years ago, the one I can tell.

You not only gave her a platform to make a big start,

But a whole new mindset to get up every time she fell.

MUSING

I know people who don't like the hustle and bustle of the city, but I can't remember how many times I must have walked that same route through the streets of London. Something about that city and its clock tower makes me feel elated. London has truly captured my heart. Perhaps it's because I remember a girl from years ago who boarded a Qatar Airways flight from Cochin International Airport to London Heathrow—a journey to the city where she wrote her story and shaped her destiny.

6

MEDITATION

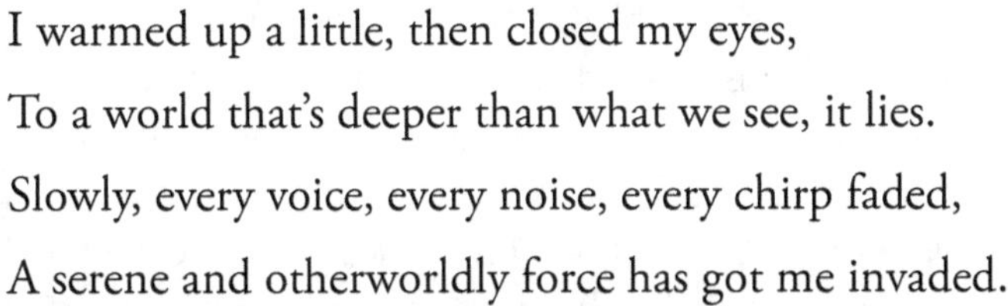

With the view of the spectacular
summer bloom,

I sat relaxed on the yoga mat in the
living room,

With my head, neck, and spine in a
straight line,

Though it took me a while to find comfort and align.

I warmed up a little, then closed my eyes,

To a world that's deeper than what we see, it lies.

Slowly, every voice, every noise, every chirp faded,

A serene and otherworldly force has got me invaded.

Why is it soothing yet more potent than I thought?

An unwinding feeling like that of a loosely tied knot.

Once holding on was the lesson we learned to grow,

But now, the uniqueness is the wisdom to let go.

Like the tranquillity of the calm waters in the sea,

Though the storm's arrival is known to all, let it be.

What keeps the mind at rest for those who are clever?

It's the understanding that nothing remains forever.

In a universe where everything moves—I love this,

The moment of stillness is the thing that I miss.

Let me enjoy this right now: the calm, the peace,

Passionately living the moments before they cease.

MUSING

We hear a lot about mindfulness, meditation, stillness, calmness, and so on—having control over our minds is one thing, but finding time to practice such sessions is another. Sometimes, we are wise enough to know our problems and solutions, but we never think about the importance of sparing some time for ourselves. I say this because I am a culprit myself. A few years back, during COVID19-, I had a personal Yoga teacher with whom I meditated. (Ironically, I had plenty of time when the world took a halt during the pandemic.) I don't often practice meditation, but when my mind is constantly on the move, I take time out on rare occasions. I wrote this poem after one such session.

7

LOVE AND WINE

Your hand drew me closer to your heart,
Imparting a feeling of not wanting to part
Amid the night and a half-conscious mind
Your soul is awake, not ready to unwind.

Don't be surprised to know what I see,
Within your arms is a place I'd love to be.
A niche-like spot is what I call it, my dear,
Where resting my head takes away my fear.

The warmth of your skin seeps into me,
With the comfort that's deeper than the sea.
Your heartbeats join mine as they leap,
Forming a tune that's unique for us to keep.

What love would be like, I did wonder once,

After a while, will it turn hostile to confronts?

But I am astonished to see what it became,

Are you eager too to know if it is the same?

Indeed, it isn't the same in quality or taste,

Nothing has improved in a matter of haste.

You know what happens to wine with age,

That should explain everything at this stage.

MUSING

Love is an emotion that sustains life. We learn each day and evolve; the same is true of love. It can only improve with time.

Love is sometimes about holding on, while other times, it is about letting go. There is no better feeling in life than love because it unravels newer meanings, deeper insights, and a greater sense of gracefulness every time we experience it. As the Scripture says, "Faith, Hope, Love—the greatest of these is Love" (1 Corinthians 13:13).

I have written about this topic many times, from many perspectives—the one I am never tired of writing and never want to be. The world needs love; I would tell everyone: "Whatever you do, do it in love."

8

COMA

The absence of light is all I remember,
And it felt like I was in a deep slumber.
I hear noises, but everything is blurry,
My words are stuck, but should I worry?

The vacuum is there, and the lack of air,
I could barely breathe, a matter to scare.
It isn't gravity, though it feels like a free fall,
Or am I being consumed by a black hole?

I am lost, and that's what people reckon.
Don't reach conclusions; wait a second.
Be patient—is all I ask till I find my voice,
And just be fair and leave me this choice.

I hear you, though very still, my body lay,

Watch your mouth and the words you say.

The day I demand answers, dear friend,

I am afraid you won't have time for a rant.

That wasn't a threat, let me assure you,

Because now I understand what is true.

It is only when you experience near-death,

You would value life to the last breath.

MUSING

I wrote the poem "Coma" inspired by Jodi Picoult's book *Wish You Were Here*. Reading the book, especially with my first-hand experience as a health professional, I connected quickly with the plot and relived the pandemic again, though not willingly. In the end, I had to write it out of my system to bring myself out of it. Have you ever felt that the stories you read remain with you for a while, lingering until you finally return to reality?

9

HOME

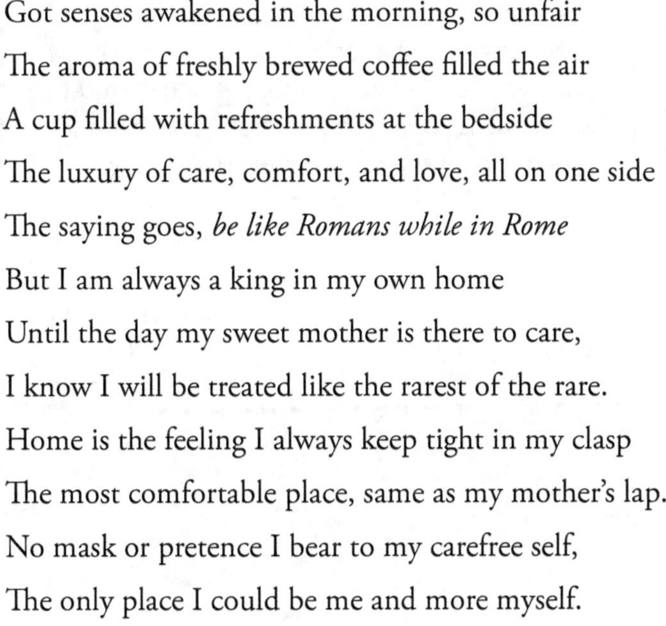

In the comfort of the crisp
white cotton bed sheet,

I couldn't resist the calls of my
beauty sleep

Got senses awakened in the morning, so unfair

The aroma of freshly brewed coffee filled the air

A cup filled with refreshments at the bedside

The luxury of care, comfort, and love, all on one side

The saying goes, *be like Romans while in Rome*

But I am always a king in my own home

Until the day my sweet mother is there to care,

I know I will be treated like the rarest of the rare.

Home is the feeling I always keep tight in my clasp

The most comfortable place, same as my mother's lap.

No mask or pretence I bear to my carefree self,

The only place I could be me and more myself.

Home is not just the place I am born and bred,

But where I hold all feelings and emotions unsaid.

No place in the world could replace my home,

My sanctuary, my haven, all under one dome.

In all I do, there is one place I wish to go back to,

Dear home, yes, I'd always be returning to you.

MUSING

No matter where you are in life, that wonderful place keeps calling you back to the confines of its comfort—one that offers you the joy of simply being yourself—that's *home*. Having a go-to place in life is a blessing that many of us take for granted. And if there are people waiting for your homecoming, that's even better. In every step we take in life, we learn to move forward, but home is the one place we cannot resist returning to. The poem "Home" portrays the love and warmth of my sweet home.

10

MORE THAN I CAN REMEMBER

A gentle breeze brushed past me,

Swaying the bushes and the leaves

It then asked a question so strange.

Tell me, my dear, you tell me now

How many lives have you touched?

More than I can remember, is all I said

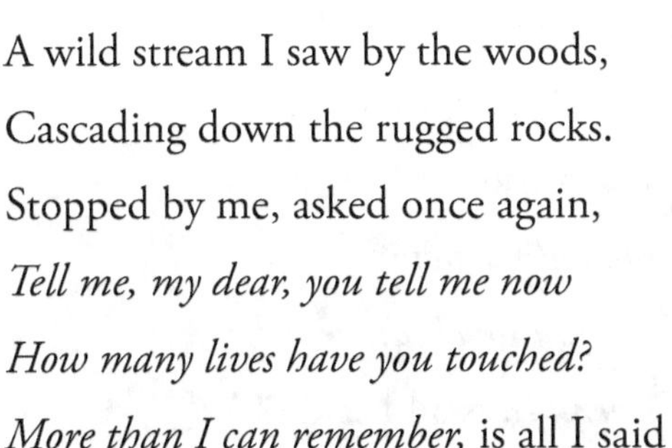

A wild stream I saw by the woods,

Cascading down the rugged rocks.

Stopped by me, asked once again,

Tell me, my dear, you tell me now

How many lives have you touched?

More than I can remember, is all I said

A goldfinch took a stop by my garden,

Sipping a drink before its next stop

She questioned me, looking into my eyes

Tell me, my dear, you tell me now

How many lives have you touched?

More than I can remember, is all I said

A dew drop sat on a petal of a plant,

Gleaming in the morning sunshine

Asked me again with its curious eyes

Tell me, my dear, you tell me now

How many lives have you touched?

More than I can remember, is all I said

A butterfly flutters, its wings around

She is dancing in joy, sipping sweet nectar.

She stops by me to ask again,

Tell me, my dear, you tell me now

How many lives have you touched?

More than I can remember, is all I said

The girl in the mirror I look at each day,

Who looks at me with a pretty smile.

Asks me proudly in her nurse uniform

Tell me, my dear, you tell me now

How many lives have you touched?

More than I can remember, is all I said.

MUSING

I am a Research Nurse by profession. I spend time with several people in my day-to-day life. To some, it's just another job, but to others, it's a calling—an opportunity to touch the lives of many. This poem is dedicated to my healthcare colleagues who make a difference in someone's life by walking the extra mile.

11

AGEING

Ageing is natural—a factual thing, dear folks,
It's not just about wrinkles and the grey locks.
Every day is a blessing when it is lived right,
But death or no life is a fact we cannot fight.

Ageing is beautiful in a poem or a storyline,
Someone said it is similar to making wine.
Though, all beautiful things come with pain.
Indeed, sometimes all our efforts go in vain.

I believe that ageing is the life in your years.
Not about all the years of your life, my dears.
Otherwise, I don't see a point in living at all,
Being part of a universe that's not-so-small.

With age comes life experiences, people say

Life keeps changing after each passing day.

In life, though, ageing has perks in many ways

Remember, in the end, it is death that prevails.

Though ageing seems a tough nut to crack,

Just make the most out of life and not slack.

Ageing happens to everyone, no matter what,

Let's not leave any regrets in life after all that.

MUSING

I talk to my parents almost every day. While busy chasing dreams, we tend to forget that with each passing day, we are growing older—and so are our parents. Though they are proud of our achievements, I feel guilty for not being present for them when they need me. I spend quality time with them through conversations over the phone— if that's the best I can do, so be it. "Ageing" is a poem born from these thoughts.

1 2

YOU WERE NEVER
<u>MEANT TO BE</u>

I thought you were on the way, as I
believed.

I prepared my life, my
heart, and my soul

I waited for you patiently,
counting the hours,

And took my every step with excellent care

But something went wrong, terribly wrong.

I called out your name and kept on and on

And I was looking for you like a mad woman

I was lost big time, and yet I didn't give up,

A wounded heart that's still raw and hurts

Though dried, the trail of my tears remains

In the end, I never found you anywhere

The truth is you never left me; what an irony!

And I learned to make peace with destiny

That maybe—you were never meant to be.

MUSING

Grieving a loss is a hard experience for anyone who has been through it. No one can fathom the pain of loss, no matter how hard they try, because the pain of loss is unique to each person. This poem pictures the traumatic story of a woman who experienced an ectopic pregnancy who, years later, somehow learned to come to terms with her loss and destiny. Some people learn to find the strength within themselves gracefully.

1 3

BETWEEN ME AND MINE (AN EXCHANGE BETWEEN ME AND MY SOUL)

I love you, I love you, my dear
soul,

You know it, you are the best of
all.

Looking at the mirror on my wall,

I said to myself who deserves it all.

With a glowing smile on my face,

That reached my eyes, in this case.

You have been kind and truthful,

And your ways are always youthful.

You are gentle like a wild stream,

Until pushed to the extreme.

In times you try not to give up,

I have seen your eyes tearing up.

Let me tell you, loud and clear,

My love for you is genuine, dear.

The tales you keep in your heart,

You've held close from the start.

I know that you don't like to spout,

But all I want is for you to let it out.

Though, at times, it all feels bleak,

I'd say just don't be afraid to speak.

Someday, you'll look back and say,

That's the best advice I got till today.

MUSING

I was fascinated by the idea of talking to oneself, which I must have picked up from a movie or a TV show. Recently, we've been hearing a lot of talk about self-love. "Between Me and Mine" is an exchange between me and my soul—my version of self-love. Be your lover and motivator, and nothing could stop you.

14

HOLD ON TO FAITH

People tell me there is no God,

And they have their own accord.

If there was a God, why the wars?

Why are there wounds and scars?

Why is there intolerance and hatred?

Why do people have to be scared?

It's true, a lot is going on out there,

Some are fair, while some are unfair.

But nothing happens out of His sight,

And He only acts when the time's right.

You can move mountains if you believe,

A promise He gave us not to deceive.

Though it may look like there is no God,

He is watching you; let's be rest assured.

Appointing His angels to guard over you,

While you are distracted by what you do.

Ours is not a world of peace, I do admit,

But then he gave us the brains to fix it.

All problems come with solutions, dear,

Let's face it by driving away our fear.

Don't be misled by people out there,

No one knows the burden they bear.

All you've to do is hold firmly to faith,

Of course, as what the scripture saith.

MUSING

We live in a world where goodness is losing its glory. We often get misleading messages, and it is easy nowadays to be misled. Holding on to faith is a reminder—that having faith doesn't mean we won't have to face adversities; it only means that we have the resilience to withstand them.

15

THE WAY TO THE CROSS—A LAMENTATION

Am I worthy of this, my dear Lord?
With the living sacrifice you served,
You gave me more than I deserved.
Am I worthy of this, my dear Lord?

Am I worthy of this, my dear Lord?
For the love you constantly pour,
And the blessings more and more.
Am I worthy of this, my dear Lord?

Am I worthy of this, my dear Lord?
For the grace you shower on me,
Significantly, the ones I fail to see.
Am I worthy of this, my dear Lord?

Am I worthy of this, my dear Lord?

To live in this world, though I dread,

You redeemed me with flesh and blood.

Am I worthy of this, my dear Lord?

Am I worthy of this, my dear Lord?

For me, to not become a lost cause,

You let your beloved son bear the cross.

Am I worthy of this, my dear Lord?

Am I worthy of this, my dear Lord?

Amazed by your love, my head I bow,

My tears couldn't help but overflow.

Am I worthy of this, my dear Lord?

MUSING

"The Way to the Cross" was written last year as a Holy Week reflection. Jesus redeemed us with blood and flesh and uplifted us from sin to be like Him. But are we holy in our ways? Are we worthy of the pain He endured? Are we living up to the worth of the price He paid? These are thoughts for self-reflection, to be worked on each day.

16

A WRITER'S MIND

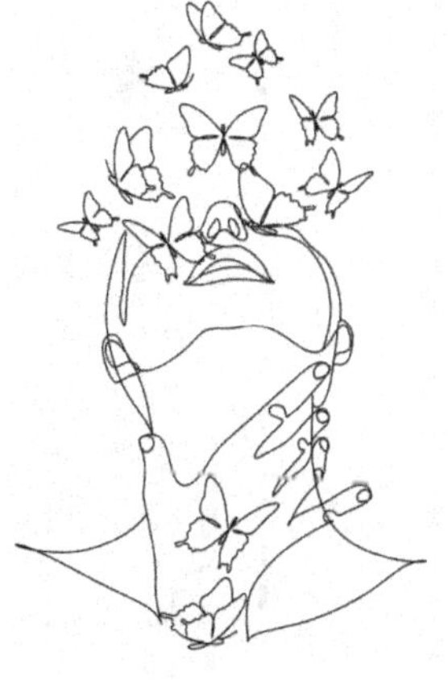

I want to write, but there is a mask
blocking my vision

I sat down, but it all felt tiring, like a
military mission.

Could it be exhaustion or the lack of
sleep, I thought,

I can't submit to this; my inner
conscience fought.

I love my mind, as it's capable of anything, so I write,

When my thoughts overflow, I don't put up a fight

I look above for inspiration and gather my words

It sets me free, with wings of its own, like the birds.

On days I am down and low, I often gather my will

So my mind could flow like a stream and not stay still

And the days I am happy, words make it even merrier

And with God beside and words within, I'm a warrior.

I don't know if writer's block is a real thing or not,

But I often have days I want to put down what I got

And some days pass by when I cannot focus one bit

But that's not enough of a reason for me ever to quit.

MUSING

"A Writer's Mind" is a poem for the writer who, one day, can't stop writing, but struggles to even find the right word on the next. Here, the writer acknowledges she has good and bad days but hesitates to believe that Writer's Block exists.

17

SOMETIMES I WISH

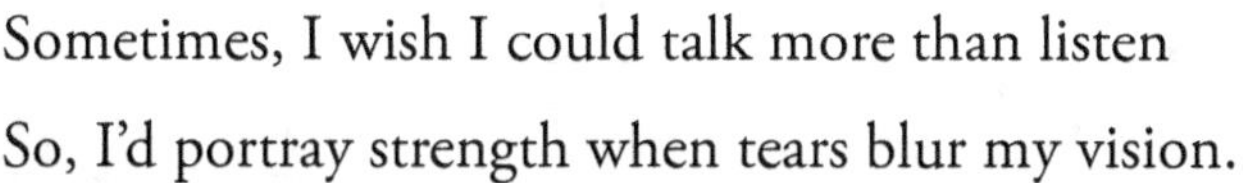

Sometimes, I wish I could learn to
hold my tears

So, I could keep away from the
world all my fears.

Sometimes, I wish I was a bit
tougher in my heart

So, I'd deal with
disappointments smoothly and smart.

Sometimes, I wish I could talk more than listen

So, I'd portray strength when tears blur my vision.

Sometimes, I wish I didn't see what I shouldn't

So, I don't have to struggle as I do to become acquaint.

Sometimes, I want the mask I wear to stay forever

So, I stay bolder before people, perfect as ever.

MUSING

The first week of 2024 has shown me different aspects of life in one frame. People from various walks of life deal with different miseries—and here I worry about how I will face and reassure them. Being a nurse is never simple. "Sometimes I Wish" is a poem that portrays the poet's struggles to mask her emotions whenever she feels the weakest.

1 8

THANK YOU, MY LORD

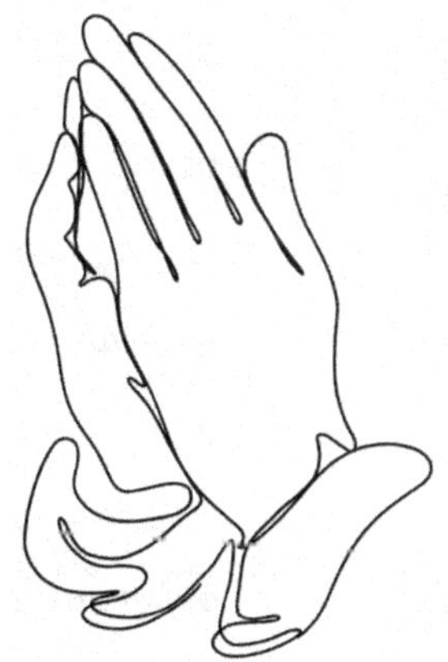

I owe thee a lot of gratitude, my Lord
For all the love you showered my way
For your grace and gifts, more than I say
I owe thee a lot of gratitude, my Lord

I owe thee a lot of gratitude, my Lord
For the best and worst, I've been through
That made us even closer, me and you
I owe thee a lot of gratitude, my Lord

I owe thee a lot of gratitude, my Lord
For my friends and family, who still stay
And for those who left my side midway
I owe thee a lot of gratitude, my Lord

I owe thee a lot of gratitude, my Lord

For my dreams and the talents bestowed by you

Reminding me how favoured I am, yes, I do.

I owe thee a lot of gratitude, my Lord

I owe thee a lot of gratitude, my Lord

For every breath of air I take in each day

And for every slight attention you pay

I owe thee a lot of gratitude, my Lord

I owe thee a lot of gratitude, my Lord

For every moment I've lived so far with you

And for those dreams yet to come true

I owe thee a lot of gratitude, my Lord.

MUSING

I wrote this poem on New Year's Eve 2023. Gratitude is a virtue; being grateful is being human. Giving thanks is not simply a greeting but an appreciation and acknowledgement of what we receive. It helps us stay grounded.

19

EDINBURGH—THE BEAUTY

Edinburgh—here I come back to you once again,

Allow me to get lost in your beautiful charm and grace

No, not because they say I am crazy and insane

But because last time, you left an imprint worth praise.

Edinburgh—you are a beauty in the winter, my love

Maybe because I haven't seen you anytime else.

In your hustling and bustling streets, we happily rove

Enveloped in your warmth and maybe those magical spells.

Edinburgh—you are home to writers and poets; I see

Indeed, it is remarkable the positivity you spread

I hope that you keep up this vibe, setting minds free

And inspiring people, though you are at it well ahead.

Edinburgh—this visit, what do you have in store for me?

I enjoy walking through the paths I walked once before

Just surprise me, that's all I would like to say to thee.

Whatever you have to offer, let me live it to the core.

MUSING

Travelling is the second-best thing I love to do after writing. Edinburgh, the Scottish capital, is home to many renowned writers and poets and the fertile ground for any person's imagination. I've always felt a magical pull towards that mystical city. Last year, we revisited the place and experienced the spirit of Christmas with a crowd that came together to share joy and good cheer. Have you ever felt that way about a place?

20

FOX'S WEDDING

I sat by the window, lost in my
thoughts,

Absorbing the warmth of the
autumn sun.

The sky was bright, then it
started raining.

Sunshine and showers; what a combo, folks!

Every time this happens, I run to the door

For a better view of the sky, for rainbows.

It does wake the child who I buried within,

It also reminds me of Grandma and her tales.

Have you been to a fox's wedding, folks?

Isn't it random—I can read your thoughts.

But that once fuelled my imagination well,

With characters from the stories I've heard.

Two foxes stood dressed up, holding hands

In Indian wedding costumes, to share vows,

The sky and the earth join the union in class,

With sunshine, rain, and a rainbow present.

Though these were tales that often repeat,

Never were they factual but harmless fiction.

What they did for sure, I know for myself,

It gave a visual animation to my own stories.

MUSING

No matter how old you become, the child within you never leaves. It was a weekend afternoon when the sunshine combined with the rain took me years down memory lane to the stories my grandmother used to tell. I dreamt of my grandmother that evening as though her presence was there. And my mom joined me with a hearty laugh. Do you still treasure those tales you heard from your grandmother?

21

GRACE UNSEEN

To the world, I am a nobody, mere dust
on the floor,

You heard that right, folks; there's
nothing more.

Every Sunday, I walk in through the
church door,

And there I see someone who loves
me to the core.

He looks at me with his face so serene and calm,

Look closely, he says, this is true, not any scam.

The cross he bore answers all the doubts I bear,

Likewise, it also drives away my worst nightmare.

It's not two pieces of wood that I see before me,

But the glory of heavens, that brings me to my knee.

Is it the abundance of grace pouring from thee?

I feel favoured in your eyes, or what could it be?

My prayers now are no longer what I want for me,

Never mind, if I am cheeky to seek your store key.

Now that I've learned your plans are better than mine,

I stay patient, though I still want to cross the line.

No matter what life throws at me, in this race,

Your divine altar keeps me content in its ways.

I can only thank you for all the unseen grace,

That keeps flowing my way from your holy place.

MUSING

In this world, where I am just one among billions of people, I am amazed by the abundance of grace and utmost care I receive from heaven above. Though we may appear too small in the universe, we didn't come about by chance; we are the work of a creator who carefully assembled this one life for each of us with accuracy and precision.

A LITTLE SURPRISE

Some of us sing, some of us dance, some of us make beautiful paintings, and some of us write. Do you know why we do what we do? It is because we have discovered the gift God has instilled in us. Not only have we found our talent, but we have also gathered the courage to pursue it. There are umpteen reasons why talents need to be recognised. It is not easy for some to come out of their comfort zone, and others may need the right people with them to appreciate those gifts. Some lack the courage, some lack the resources, and some lack the support. As we grow, we uplift each other on our journey—that's what life is all about.

On the next page, I have a beautiful surprise for you.

IT'S ALL UP TO YOU...

—*Diya Anna Binsily*

If I told you to meet me in
the stars beneath the sky
Would you follow me through
the darkness?
If you do so, I will give you
the light you thrived for
Not just once or twice, but
Forever.

If I told you, you must meet me
Would you come?
And if you come, I promise.
You will be happier…
But you said it isn't up to
me
It's all up to you…

Diya is a creative 8-year-old with a passion for writing. Ever since she started reading, she has been captivated by stories and has now begun crafting her own tales and poems. She enjoys reading, dancing, crafting, and other similar pursuits when not writing.